Di Achichúk

Di Achichúk

POEMS AND IMAGES FROM BATANES

Dorian S. Merina

bughaw

Published by BUGHAW

BUGHAW is an imprint of
Ateneo de Manila University Press
Bellarmine Hall, ADMU Campus
Loyola Heights, Katipunan Avenue
Quezon City, Philippines
Tel.: (632) 426-59-84 / Fax (632) 426-59-09
E-mail: unipress@ateneo.edu
Website: www.ateneopress.org

Cover design by Nikki Solinap
Book design by Paolo Tiausas

The National Library of the Philippines CIP Data

Recommended entry:

Merina, Dorian S.
Di Achichúk : poems and images from Batanes / Dorian S. Merina. -- Quezon City : Bughaw : an imprint of Ateneo de Manila University Press,[2019], c2019.
xiv, 94 pages; 21.59 cm

ISBN 978-971-550-921-3

1. Philippine poetry (English) I. Title.

899.2101   PR9550.9.M47   P920190101

For m, x and c
you
who set my heart free

And for those who left
those who stayed
those who return

CONTENTS

III.

PREFACE

After a day at sea, fishermen in our village often gather in a circle to divide the catch. We squat low on the ground, arms dripping with seawater. One of us rinses a knife and slits the belly of a fish. Another grabs a spoon and, using its edge, scrapes the tough scales and fins. There's a lot of laughter, jokes, teasing, and storytelling. This is called *atatayen*, dividing the catch, when everyone gets their share of the day's work and each person's contribution is recognized. You may also find someone drawing out a glass of *palek*, the native sugarcane wine, to start a song amid the chopping and cleaning.

Lipus ko am panahanen ko ava du payhudhuran
ta riyalen nu araw, ta riyalen nu araw.

I don't make my relative pass on the hill's ridge
for there the sun shines down brightly.

These lines are from a Laji, the oral poetic tradition of Batanes. It's a tradition that has been passed down through generations. Lajis can be funny or tragic, celebratory or mournful. They spin tales, recount village events, and express longing and joy. I have spent many hours during these past fifteen years or so seeking out the last elders here on the islands who know these songs, recording and transcribing their voices and talking to them about how they learned their art and where it comes from. Though it is a tradition constantly in danger of vanishing, I do not learn the songs for the sake of nostalgia. Rather, I believe our contemporary world—with its challenges and forgetfulness—is in need of this artistic imagination, these rare and valuable phrases that express a particular way of living, a specific balance with the natural world. They are gifts from our ancestors, who were also flawed, also full of dreams, also brilliant in their own way.

Batanes is the northernmost province of the Philippines, located in the deep channels where the Pacific Ocean meets the China Sea. It is remote and has been for many generations, yet it has also been a crossing point for people from what today is Taiwan, to the north, and Indonesia, to the southwest. It is home to the Ivatan, the indigenous community that has made the rough seas and volcanic hills their home since before national boundaries were drawn.

It is also where my family is from and where we live today.

The poems in this collection, *Di Achichúk*, draw on this tradition. Most were composed orally during the winter, *amyan*, and rainy season, *kachachimuyen*, that dictate the daily life on these remote shores. They follow the cycle of planting and fishing, the seasons and the tides. They evolved over time, were shared with others, only later coming to the page in written form. Some tell collective stories, such as the exile of Ivatan people during the eighteenth century, while others explore personal themes, like the birth of my daughter. Many began as lines I would repeat aloud as I made my way from our home to our small farm along the shore, with just the wind as my companion.

Yet the poems, like my own background, spring also from other influences, such as the literary and artistic traditions of Latin America and Southeast Asia, the Carribbean and Native North America. I can still hear, with great pleasure, the limericks and ballads my mother's German-Irish parents would recite to us as children. And I'm still moved by the energy and excitement of the 1990s hip-hop and spoken word scene of Los Angeles, where I spent my teenage years. In those days, I often sought out the latest albums from De La Soul or 2Pac or Native Guns, while also listening to my grandmother's tales of life in Batanes, where a giant rock marked the gateway to her small village. Her stories described a time before motorized boats, before electricity, before even the global war that would profoundly reshape our countries, the Philippines and the US, and my own family.

Many years later that giant rock also marks the boundaries of my own home, and those of my neighbors, in the small village of Savidug. It also names the collection of poems you now hold in your hands.

So imagine that you are here beside us in this circle, still catching your breath from the quick jog from the shore. Your arms are damp with sea spray. *Maydisna ka dya*. I have a few stories, a few songs, a few poems to share with you.

You probably have your own, too.

Dorian S. Merina
Savidug, Batanes, Philippines
February 2019

Di Achichúk

PROLOGUE

There is a story
about how some
of the people
disappeared beneath
the big rock in the ocean.
Maybe there was a door
made of stone
or a secret passage
or one of the deep pools
turned out not to have
a bottom
down below.
This part of the story
we don't know

the old man tells me
as he slices ginger
in the doorway.

We also don't know
what they found
when they went down there
or why they went
but one day
someone spotted them
from up on the hill
near the field

where you now plant
your crops.
And when they emerged
their hair was long
and gray
which was different
from before.
Their eyes were wide
and open
but they did not speak.
In fact,
they were silent
a long time.

The old man
he pauses
to catch his breath
or maybe to harness
his strength for what
comes next.

It is just a story
he says
but listen closely
you need to know
what happened.

I.

INHERITANCE

Others have cleared
this field
before

where grass gives way
to dark mineral clay
and white sea rocks.

This morning I find
goat scat
and clumps of damp dirt

beneath the *asada's* blade,
slicing into earth
after days of rain.

From this height you can see
the other islands beyond
the rolling ocean

and to the south
the ancient fortress
beneath the mountain

where our ancestors
retreated in times of risk
and danger

and also
these hills are where

they fought during the war
hiding in the shadows
and the night wind

until foreign soldiers seized them
including Lola's two brothers
still boys

and brought them
down from the hills
to the town

to ensure there were
witnesses around
when they drove

bayonets into their chests.

That was the time
of the Japanese
and cruelty

was a coiled snake
ready to strike
and pounce again.

Before that the Americans
before that the Spanish
even our own hands

cunning with power
could devour our most
precious promise

and leave us lost
in a whirlwind
within our own homes.

I pull the grass
into bundles
small enough

for my arms to lift
and carry
to the border.

If there is enough earth
the weight is like
my child

whom I hold
and rock at night
coaxing her to sleep and dreams

with songs that seem
to find each other's verse
line by line.

There is a storm coming
you can see it in the distance.
Before I reach

the path home
my shoulders will be
drenched with rain.

CUTTING BAMBOO

First you need a sharp knife
so wet the stone
and tone the blade
until it sings across the air

then find the path
around the hillside
by the tree line
and down into the grove
where you will spend
the afternoon
among the shadows
and tall grass.

Choose wisely
which stems to cut
smooth and slender
the rings of dried leaves
already blown free.

If the moon is waning
arrive early
while the dew is fresh
and the ground damp and soft

or expect a scolding from Aunty
who warns that the next
generation of grass
will not grow back.

One strike against the base
should separate the root
but take care
not to bruise the young shoots
growing there

let them fall into a pile
that shakes and rustles in the wind
you still must clean the sides
and slice the knuckles bare
and tie the load and hoist it
to your shoulders
to climb the steep hill once more

so take your time
allow the afternoon to pass
to later hours of the day
when evening air approaches
and drifts down cool
from high in the mountains

the sun now turning gold
and getting lost
among the leaves.

Yayu

AYUB

Her arms always had more to hold
a child on the cusp of sleep
she cradles me now my nose
pressing against her chest's skin breathing in
the odor of breastmilk and sweat
another arm pulling the curtain loose
to allow in afternoon light another
child wrestling free another on the way

she was raised alone taken home
to rooms quiet as canvas stretched
across floorboards absorbing
steps as light as breath

when we arrived she was a young woman
newly into adulthood from an island
far away from here and left
on faith or perhaps something more

in those days you did
what you had to do which meant
she always said that sometimes
you make something out of nothing

like an *ayub* out of love
the edges soft and smooth tucked
beneath sleeping limbs

a knee an elbow a foot

there were other times when love
alone was not enough
to keep the rush at bay
it's hard to recall those days now
even with you in my arms
your grandparents so young holding
the days together around them
like us now in a way

wind runs over the ocean
and comes down the mountain
to the village the temperature falls

what I need I think
is a blanket soft and warm
to tuck beneath your chin
an armament of stars that sets
the night's new directions free
as I bend near and kiss
your forehead clean

LULLABY

Go to sleep, my child
my child, go to sleep

for the future
we cannot see

even you who peers
into the shadows in the rafters

and I who still
can hear the voices

of those who passed
from this world

as I held their hands in mine
and knelt by their side

their breathing ragged and slow
as death approached

your grunts grow firm
from birth to struggle

how do we know
the difference
when the breath
breaks free

So sleep my child
the wind

after a day of rattling
is calm

and the almond tree
by the window

holds its leaves
no longer

as if it waited for just this moment
to send them

spinning into the dark

Vuchid

NIGHT WIND

Listen to this night wind
shaking the boughs like
seabirds skidding across stones.

It could mean tomorrow
there will be no *bangka*
to make the crossing

instead left stranded on the beach
the motor cold and still
in the dark salt air.

It could also mean my love
will sleep past dawn
then rise

draw down the bedsheet
to descend the stairs
and run water through her hands her cheeks

a slight shiver
at her temples

before rubbing coconut oil
across her still-warm belly
turning it clear from milky white.

And you, my child
asleep to man's
strict schedules and schemes

will you cry
startled by the wind's
sudden roar?

Or will it soothe
your dreams
the memories

of your ancestors
still circling just beyond
your sharp vision—

and maybe another cause and effect
I have not yet
worked out

another spirit cast
far and wide
by the night wind's capricious path.

Kawayan

AT THE FIELD EDGE

At the field edge
the red clay shards
gather like fish scales in the rain

how many years
my ancestors
pressed their feet

into the limestone
to carry the earth vessels
up this hill

water
sugarcane liquor
animal fat eased into their arms

as they navigate the steep incline
ocean waves pounding
just below.

They say
when the jar broke
they abandoned it in the field

to slowly sink back
into the grit and bone
of the hillside

the ancient bedrock
still shaped by the sea
until generations hence

my blade glances off
the packed crust of guava roots
underground grass shoots and loam

the pottery still smooth
against a human hand
cupped its memory tumbles out

what once held time now timeless
a fragment broken
to become complete

STONES

So this is what concrete
looks like after twenty years
when it is unfinished
and battered by storms

I was a young man
when it was poured
though in a different land
a different place

now face to face
out my back window
in this small village
by the sea

and see
I keep wanting to say:
even stones become air
eventually

Khali After Dancing

CROSSING

Rain covers the mountains in mist

The *bangka* slices the dark ocean with white foam

We depart before dawn
masari pa
the smell of sea salt and
rain clouds on the wind

I have made this crossing many times

Some days the waves as high as houses
or the surface as smooth as the sky
and always
the strong current
pushing and tossing
the boatsides
on the journey east

This morning I rise in the dark
kiss my child's face
eyes wide and sleepy
mayvidi aku andelak
I will return tomorrow

And now the day is taking shape

The island expanding
on the horizon
beach sand coming
into view

A column of gray smoke against the green hills

YARU

We hammer wood into old planks
of the church. The place of prayer

now filled with men with long knives
strapped to their waists.

I stand on pews reaching up
into the eaves to fasten braces.

Someone pulled the stations of the cross
off the walls and stacked them
in the rectory,

the wooden pegs now bare
and framing air where once foretold
the story of spirit and its ascent
from stone and pain.

After days of rain
sudden sunlight outside
so we comment on the change
and goats and cows in the fields,
December planting
and the crops still to be put in.

These days I remember
the ones who have passed on,
some after long lives
others too soon and hard to fathom,
the sunder of flesh from bone.

After the day of work
I sit at home my child in my arms.
She is not yet forty days in this world
so we talk of spirits
as the sky gets dark. The wind
as always in this season
whistles off the stone walls
and shakes the grass roof.

After this another day
a sun a moon
the rumination of our kiss
into the earth.

We return to work and prayer
summoned to this place
our memories lifting skyward
our dreams here to stay.

Sa Kusina

PLOWING

All morning my neighbor
in the next field
carves a constellation into earth,

the grunt and strain
of man and beast
plowing the ancient seabed.

Through the brush I can hear
the slap against skin
and sweat.

Nearby there is a hill
where our ancestors
carved holes into stone posts
and cleared the ground
above the ocean
the closest height to stars
on moonless nights.

A stone path
by the river
takes you there

past other fields
and pools of rainwater
gleaming in the shadows.

By afternoon we are both gone
back to the village
and our children and homes,

the fields unfinished
and torn open
as night comes.

MAYOR:
Mariano "MAR" Gabito
VICE MAYOR:
Clemente "MEMEN" Ladreza
SB MEMBER:
Aranda, Angelita
"ANGIE"
Cabalda,
"TONY"
Cervillon, Juliana
"JULING"
Faberes,
"DELING"
Cultura, Eden
Loreto,
Triliana, Roberto
"BERT"

Roofing

PRAISE

The newborn goat crouches
in the mouth of the cave

the short hair on its rump
brown as the brown on the sandstone cliffs

all morning the rain falls and falls

the red throat of the rooster
bounces up and down
as it prowls the yard next door
the damp tan sand
matches its trident feet

How will the firewood dry now?
And what of the bamboo poles
stacked on river stones?
Or even: where do these birdsongs
finally come to rest
after days of calling?

all morning the rain falls and falls

Andelak means tomorrow
or maybe the next day
and sometimes even
never

Nearby mother and child are singing
in the loft
you have just cut a plate
of fresh red onions
and the scent is slicing the air
one or two tomatoes from the field
are spilling their seeds
into the small bowl
and the eggs from the next village
crack softly in your hand
yolk bursts forth
in its yellow hue
and there's nothing
left to do but praise

EMPTY

With this wind
the beach is empty
the fishermen are home

my own spear hangs
above the wood stove
on brass hooks
beside a braid of smoked garlic

I imagine the fish
beneath the churning waves
darting and dashing
by the rocks we hold
to steady our shoulders
against the fast current

they wake
and sleep
and wake again
and also wait
for the sun to break the surface
and illuminate the blades of sea grass
rising from ivory sand

When we meet again
the terms will be the same
I will swim with a single purpose
and so will they

but today

the sky is heavy with clouds
so let us live
and be free
and admire our beautifully
shaped bodies our tough
and tender skin

our minds washed clean of memory
as if tomorrow's sun comes
just once
to unweave the dawn's dark vest
and fill the world
with light

Miss Gay Talisay 2018

CHRYSANTHEMUMS

I slice the stem
of the chrysanthemum
with my machete,

wet earth
clings
to the blade.

We carry the bouquet
across the village,
the bright flowers
singing with yellow petals.

Our old neighbor passed
just after New Year's
and now she lies
in the *sala* of her home

as family and friends
gather in plastic chairs
with their backs
against the open window.

I stand by the doorway,
sandals heavy with field stones
and black dirt,
but can hear the stories

and answer back
to laughter
when they joke
about my plowing
and how the body tires
from working the steep slopes.

Her son brings light
into homes,
dipping his hands
into thick concrete walls
to arrange the wires
so the power flows
from dark to light.

In our own house it was
during a storm
when he came,
our arms and backs slick
with sweat and rain,
flashlights swinging like stars
through the dark rooms.

Now he sits
by the casket,
the chrysanthemums
on the table by his elbow.
He is quiet beside the bright
yellow petals
of the flowers.

LAJI

Deep memories steeped
in ox teeth and ash.
The corn rows lined
with coral and clay shards.

These hills are named
for people or animals
who met a fate
memorable enough
to commemorate in song.

What I recall
the lines and melody
taught to me
by an old woman
who was killed
in her home
by a neighbor who got drunk
and wouldn't leave.

We heard the story first
at the port
when we arrived

an uncle from the next village
the one who knows
the old way of roofing
told us what had happened
when we were gone

but he only knew a little
and kept repeating
in a way that made me realize
you would no longer be there
when we reached
the island

our sorrow unending
in the ceaseless wind.

With each telling
each teller revealed
a new piece
of what had happened.

She survived the attack
and lasted part of the night
so the telling was hers
at first.

I light a candle
in the open window
at night. Its thick flame
flickers against the dark hills.

You sang each line
and took time to explain
the lyrics: when a phrase
means envy, for instance,
or fish swimming or
love even the kind that's hard
to define.

She was the last
singer in the village
who knew the songs
from long before.

The words were often metaphors
with double meanings

like the fish baskets
we drag to the shallows
of the sea. Their mouths woven
to let the flashing silver bodies through

knife-blade fins held taut
against the current

but not to leave.

Di Jidaúd

NIGHTFALL

Ina shushes baby
from the table
where she peels back
garlic skin with her thumb

the purple membranes collect
at her elbow
trembling in the breeze.

Through the open doorway
a chicken with feathers
as brilliant as sunrise dashes
to peck at the red tiles

the baby's eyes widen
dark like the wet earth of the hillside
after rain.

And where is Ama

coming home from the farm
thin straps of the *kalapay* pressing
against his shoulders
the load is not too heavy: a handful of okra
eggplant, green tomatoes, and a bag
of hot chili peppers. He left

the bundle of wood
fastened with the *rayi*
for tomorrow.

Today he takes the path
by the shoreline
back to the stone house.

When he arrives
his sandals are covered
with chalk dust
and cow dung from the field
and he places

the sun now sinking into the hills

his kisses gently on his daughter's cheek
his wife's face
dusk and the beating heart of nightfall
still to come.

II.

ACHICHÚK

Ichasi mu pa yamen mu, Kasi.
Have mercy on us, Kasi.

i.

The rock finds me and the old man
          talking about the rock we have lived
between us well over one hundred twenty years
          yet there is so much we do not know like
how did you break away from the mountain
          and fall into the ocean and why did you rise
from the seafloor to seek the world above
          and how do you float on the surface of the waves
even amid the billowing sheets of heavy rain

ii.

Up close the sharp rock is porous and the color of rust
          the *kayang* flee like shadows into narrow crevices
you are suddenly surrounded by the deeper sea
          the shoreline in the distance the stone homes hidden
by coconut trees a narrow road rises from the beach
          high to fields covered in mist in the hills
the only thing you can hear: wave after wave
          sinking into the rock as each one brings what it has carried
from the depths to its restless destination

iii.

One afternoon three goats nibble on green grass at the peak
          from the distance their backsides
slope against the sky like the mountains
          on the other island across the sea
they stay the whole afternoon while waves crash
          below another day they are gone
the grass remains the rock the waves the sky beyond
          the constant roar and swell that hide the path
up jagged steps from tide pools far below

iv.

The rock is often the first thing you see
          when coming home from a trip far away
or a brief day working the fields
          it never looks the same yet is always there
marking the point on the breakwater
          where the land turns sharper north
then runs to open sea from far away a shimmer
          in the haze the ships that drift
from distant cities then in the night disappear

v.

A styrofoam boat lashed with vines to help it float
          there is a gap between the rock shelf and the hillside
high above the shore on dry land the distance
          ten thousand fathoms of light
air and wind rushing past the dunes
          a lone plastic bottle bounces lightly at low tide
a blue crab shell rattles on the stones and finds
          a place to rest an empty home made vacant by the wind
as sand passes through and scrapes the hillside dry

vi.

Depending on the tide
          it is a refuge or a landbridge
a path out into the sea or a cave of deep
          whirling pools that sinks into the earth
depending on the tide the sides rise in great
          walls of stone the ring of water
suddenly smooth as glass shades of green and coral
          clear or shattered in tumultuous noise
depending on the tide

vii.

I have asked everyone here who has a memory
        of the time before about this rock
nakayapu kaychuwa they say *from long long ago*
        they all know a story how I would fish
by the rocks so that when mama called we could hear
        her voice from the grove or even about the Americans
who planted a flag of course at its top during occupation everyone
        has a story but no one reveals the origins so I change
my questions to harbor longer lives

viii.

The blue digger sits by the side of the road
        its arm bent and covered in rust
from the rock the machinery is small and nearly
        lost against the hillside was it abandoned
this blue digger or simply left behind another piece of progress
        lost to the excavation of time
and now a white heron perches on its roof feet dripping wet
        a moment ago it waded through pools
at the rock's base before lifting in flight

ix.

If you dive into the water near the rock's walls
		you will see from beneath the waves
the sky churning far above
		the fish know all about this world
and when the storms unleash their spirits
		from over the ocean they seek
the secret pools where it is dark and still
		it's easy to get lost swimming
among the rocks and seagrass sky and wind

x.

How many generations have we peered
		at the curving rock and the clouds beyond
there is a word for it this journey in our language
		it comes also from this land these hills
this memory and means to leave and then return
		with different dreams and years behind them
sometimes the stories told are familiar other times they're lost
		an echo circling back in the wind
it starts and always ends right here

Achichúk, Makuyab

III.

EXILE

They were exiled
for half a century
from the island

the ocean became
a deep and treacherous
border cut into the land.

The punishment imposed
by Spanish officials
a consequence for insurrection
certain as the fine embroidery
on the priest's frock ironed hot
and flat for mass.

                    Even so
some were driven back
by hunger or loneliness
to the green hills
and the damp forests
but always to leave
by nightfall
with dreams of home
fading like salt spray
against the boatsides.

When it was finally over
many did not return
for the passage of time
takes its toll
and heartbreak runs through
generations like
a thirst quenched by water
pulled from the bitter gourd.

The ones who did return
gathered stones and lime
from the shoreline
brought down wood from the hills
and built the homes
where we now live.

This was all more than one hundred eighty years ago
and tonight
look how the first-quarter moon
fills the town streets
with glowing light,
the sky filled with stars
and clouds and wind.

We are still named
for the tree
lodged into the hillsides
its broad leaves turning dark red when
the rainy season nears its end,
inside green teardrops
new leaves wait silently
to open.

Banda du Timbaan

ON THE WAY HOME

Feet braced against river stones
we fill plastic jugs
with water for pigs crops goats

evening light ripples
on the pool

no rain for days
just sun and wind
turning the topsoil white
with sand and coral

On the way home
I turn and climb the dunes
from behind the shoreline stretches south
waves pull themselves free
from deep sea to crash
over rocks and roll past the breakwater

Nearby stone markers press
into the earth
arranged into a hull
barely wide enough for a man
folded on his side
to find and hold the bow
always pointed east and to the sea
along this rise

The evening darkens
wind whips the rain pants on my shins
clattering the machete at my hip until

I turn to walk the rest of the road
to the village and home

MOONLIGHT

All night the cows
in the next lot
do their mischief
in the moonlight.

Aunty always loosens
the rope
on the tall black steer
and the rest follow,

their broad
shoulders
heaving muscles
uphill.

And now they're cracking
branches under hooves
and chewing at the gatesides
of the old stone house.

In the morning they are gone,
the sunlight drying dew drops
on the bruised necks
of tall grass.

Mayatep

LAMAY

Another death in the village
two nights ago
as the full moon grew
from behind clouds

the dead man's son
comes to our house
and sits on the wall
in the front yard

still a boy
he asks shyly
for flowers from among the rocks
by the door

I gather a handful
and offer them
with the scissors still
in my hand

he clasps the dark green leaves
some buds not yet open
and sits there
looking sideways.

We ask what happened
though we all witnessed
the man's dark wanderings
in the bright daylight

the watery eyes locked
far beyond the mountains

An illness, says the boy.

The mourning begins
at sunset and lasts
for nine days
while the soul seeks solace
the living peace.

BUTCHERING

The butchering begins before dawn
dry grass gathered and lit
to a bright red ember

machetes whistle in the dark

sending a spray of sparks skyward
to dance into the stars
a cellphone erupts in song
and shines a blue light
into the shadows

Nearby the pig is tied to the tree
and grunts and struggles
against the ropes
soon four men
grasp the beast into their arms
and pull
coarse hair straining against the skin

the knife is plunged
at the throat
eyes wide and open
then shut
and quiet

the crackle of flame
and smoke roasting
the spines of coconut branches
slit fat at the stems

morning breaks into the clearing
softly
slowly
where life was taken

Sentro Port

GATHERING

When we gathered mussels
the shallows were hot
against our feet

malawang

low tide stretched long and wide

Little Jim and little Gab
splashed from rock to rock
and carried in their cupped hands
the curved creatures
and bits of sand and seaweed
to fill the plastic pails

Early morning
but the sun's glare
against the bare patches
of the sea
already
making us squint through T-shirts
tied across our eyes

You have to feel
carefully
with your fingers
beneath the underside of rocks
in the warm pools

the work is slow
and so the kids
told stories
and we did too

the morning passed that way
the shoreline fine and far away

SINGS

the worm
wants to live

as does the snake
　　　gliding through the shade
　　　　　　of the green reeds

and the bird high
　　　in the boughs
　　　　　　of the breadfruit tree

and you and me
　　　with our busy minds
　　　　　　spinning desire into dreams

she sings
　　　the bird
　　　　　　across the open field

and nearby
　　　there comes
　　　　　　an answer

he waits
　　　the snake
　　　　　　along the cleared field

and nearby
    a machete
        swings free

past the thicket
    by the path beaten flat
        by footsteps

in the nook of a tree
    the worm shakes loose its casing
        of leaves and damp soil

it is a struggle
    as many days
        will be

yet there is also
    an ease
        when the rain falls

lightly
    and soaks
        the fields

and a breeze
    passes through
        lifting briefly

each leaf to the sky
each life to earth

Misa

THE CATCH

We catch three fish
with silver hooks that gleam
like the sun

they leap into the boat
thrashing in the ropes
their blue bellies
send sea spray across the deck

high waves push the boat
from side to side
the motor slows but doesn't cease

they gasp and breathe
their bodies as long
as a man's arm

this is the part of the ocean
where both shores
seem to recede
into the distance

and the sky opens
with white light

three lines drawn
across the chest
winding round and round
the steel wheel again

A QUESTION

I can watch the waves
crash along the shore

from our window
upstairs

It is a small view
past the arching trunks

of the coconut trees
not like one of those

horizon to horizon vistas
you see in magazines

But it is enough
to know

if it is a good day to fish
or cross to the next island

and it gives me
something to say

when I find my neighbor
snapping branches
off the *aryaw* tree
for his goats

after all
what would I do with more

what would you?

Savidug vs. Sumnanga

SECOND PLANTING

We pull back the tough weeds
beneath the *hangu* tree,
scrape the carabao dung
with our blades

fill two pails
with rich earth.

Low clouds and a light wind
on the horizon.

The patch of field
beyond the tree line
is ready
for the second planting.

I will dig manure
into the sandy soil
and gather water
from the rain barrel,
sifting leaves and insects
with my hands.

In town the streets
are busy
these days
before our *pyesta*.

A ring of green reeds
and flowers frame
the main road.
The elders stoop and sweep
the gutters free of debris,
stiff bristles brushing
against the stone.

          But we are near the fields now

and kneel beside
an empty road.

          From over the dunes
          the ocean rolls and roars,
          goats amble and bay
          teeth tugging
          at wildflower roots.

Pails heavy
I head to the forest
along the dry river
balancing each footstep
as I go.

PYESTA

Here come the drums
beating in the streets

mawara da na sa
mawara da na sa

araw nu pyesta
du dekey a barrio namen aya

Here come the drums
the children dance over damp stones
red sashes flashing at their waists

Here come the drums
and the procession of candle flames
held beneath chins in a half-moon light

Antiyaw mangay kamu du vahay namen
later come to our home
past the open doorways
where woodsmoke and garlic oil
drift from busy kitchens

we will fill a *kabaya* leaf with food
and not let you leave
until you are happy and full

so come and stay
mangay kamu dya
mangay kamu dya

It is the day of our *pyesta*
the streets are full
and the drums are coming

Three Kings

DOGS, BIRDS

Two dogs
chase birds
across the sand dunes

morning sun breaks
through the clouds and lights up
the white fur on their hind legs.

A soft wind carries
their yelps
to the open road

the dogs are fast
and dash from one dune
to the next

but the birds
are faster
and fly high into the sky.

Sumla

BY THE RIVER

Everyone else is at mass
getting the cross
traced in damp ash
across their forehead

I am kneeling by the river
the one dry in summer
today holds cool pools
stirred by carabao hooves
as their massive bodies sink
into the dark water

It is quiet
and yes the sun is here
and the wind
and the red ant crawling
from stone to stone
light to dark

the *vutalao* tree casts
its shower of fine roots
from a branch on the muddy bank
they fall between rocks
and the river bottom and sway
in the languid current

the bird arrives
and pierces the shadow
with its flight
its call follows close behind

these are the holy days
when we dare offer prayers
for all that is taken and given
and I am watching this water
course down to the sea
from forest and green hills
through rock and root

Now it is time to go
but I linger
composing my song
I drift
and think of you

NOTES

Prologue

Leslie Marmon Silko's novel, *Ceremony*, and the story of Tayo and the Laguna people has returned to me many times over the years. Silko's work has helped me think about how, as both a migrant and an indigenous person, I can tell my story and why it's worth it. This prologue is, in part, an homage to her profound work. Special thanks also to Lolo Valiente Horcajo.

Inheritance

During World War II, the island of Sabtang was the center of guerrilla resistance in Batanes. Many young Ivatan people were killed by Japanese forces for taking part in the fighting or for merely being suspects. My grandmother's younger brothers, Alejandrino and Eladio Canela, were two of those killed by the Japanese. Today, there is a small monument in Sinakan, near Sabtang's port, commemorating some of the victims.

The ancient hilltop fortresses, known as idjangs in Ivatan, are shrouded in mystery. There are more than a dozen of them located throughout Batanes. In at least one case, the Itbud Idjang, Ivatans used the fortress to launch a revolt against the Spanish. (The revolt at Itbud took place in 1789 and is documented by Dr. Cesar Hidalgo in the *Ivatan-Filipino-English Dictionary*, p. 188.)

Ayub

Ayub is the Ivatan word for blanket, or covering.

Laji

As I note in the preface, Laji is the traditional Ivatan form of oral poetry. This poem is dedicated to LFH, who lived in Savidug and taught me the lajis she had learned from her elders as a young woman. For more, see Dr. Florentino Hornedo's essential study, *Laji: Nu Maddaw Ka Mu Lipus, An Ivatan Folk Lyric Tradition*, and our ongoing documentation and recordings at www.ivatanlaji.org.

Achichúk

Ichasi mu pa yamen mu, Kasi is a traditional prayer used by fishermen when setting out to the ocean. According to Hornedo, kasi is the ancient term for arayu, the migratory, deep-sea fish that is a staple of the Ivatan fishing season. Hornedo also says that the prayer could have its origins in ancient invocations to an ocean diety. (See "Fishing the Traditional Ivatan Way," by Hornedo in his book,*Taming the Wind*.)

This poem went through many manifestations on its way to its current form. I am indebted to the following writers, whose own work provided guidance in form and structure: Leslie Marmon Silko (*Storyteller, Almanac of the Dead*); Joy Harjo (*A Map to the Next World*); W.S. Merwin (*Folding Cliffs, The Shadow of Sirius*); and Eduardo Galeano (*Memoria del Fuego, Bocas del Tiempo*).

The spelling, Achichúk, is my best approximation of the name for the giant rock, which is known only through oral tradition. It's possible that other spellings may be just as valid.

Exile

After a deadly uprising against the Spanish in 1791, Aman Dangat, Sabtang's traditional chieftain, was tried by the Spanish colonial government and killed. Other leaders were punished and the island's residents were forcibly removed to Ivana, a village on Batan island. There they remained for fifty years, until the exile was officially ended in 1844 under the new Spanish mission post of Fr. Antonio Vicente.

On The Way Home

Boat-shaped burial markers, made of stone, can be found near shorelines throughout Batanes. Traditional Ivatan practice was to bury loved ones beneath stones in the shape of boats, facing toward the sea. Erosion and shifting land have exposed some to the elements. Others have been the subject of ongoing archaeological research by teams of Ivatan and Filipino academics. (See Eusebio Z. Dizon and Jun Cayron's "Archaeological Excavation of a Stone Boat-Shaped Burial No. 7 at Locality I, Nakamaya, San Antonio, Basco, Batanes," and Grace Barretto, Armando Salvador B. Mijares, and Rey Santiago's "Preliminary Exploration of the Vatang Stone Boat-Shaped Marker and San Vicente Idjyang, Ivana, Batan Island, Batanes Province," in the *Ivatan Studies Journal*, Volume V–X, 1998–2003, SCBI Graduate School Research Journal.)

Savidug weaving design

The black-and-white pattern found in the section breaks is my own hand-drawn interpretation of a traditional Savidug weaving pattern. It is inspired by a particular *vuvud*, or jewelry basket, woven by Gregorio Hontomin, resident of Savidug, circa 1930. Thanks to Paolo Tiausas at Ateneo University Press for designing the layout with creativity and care.

ACKNOWLEDGMENTS

To the spirits before me for their wisdom, kindness and courage: Maria Canela, Catalino Cassanova, Rose Keil Turk, Edward Joseph Turk, Cristina Conde, Al Macdonald, Uncle Quilino, Lola Filomena, Alejandrino and Eladio Canela.

To the *kataysas* for always offering their time, despite everything, to help me find the right word and the truth behind it: Anastacia Merina, Ireneo Canela and Sheryl Hornedo, Roland Gabilo. Thanks also to Vicenta Hidalgo for discussing with me the finer points of Ivatan language at a critical point in the editing.

To the *marans* and *kamnans* for making sure the farms are plentiful, the garlic is braided and the stories continue: Julian and Ollette, Antonino and Fortunata, Ursula, Antonio and Remy, Inocensia. *Matakaw ava diyaten u kasulivan.*

To my sisters, for accompanying me on this journey with love, humor and encouragement: Vanessa Alexandra, Hilary Rose Canela, Kali Emelia Keil.

To my brothers, for always being there for me, across distance and time: Genai Kerr, Rudy Mangual, Drew Rice, Diego Carmona.

To my fellow poets, trespassers and dreamers, for showing that beauty and imagination still matter in this crazy world: Irene Suico Soriano, Allan Aquino, David Gramling, Pat Payne, Alison de la Cruz, Alwin Alguirre,

Luis H. Francia, Cherry Muhanji . . . and the artists and energies behind the Balagtasan Collective, LA Enkanto, and FPAC (Festival of Philippine Arts and Culture).

To my fellow journalists for doing the tough work of truth-telling, often at great risk and against all odds: Sheila Coronel, Alisa Solomon, Catherine Komp, Shannon Young, Nell Abram, Vinod K. Jose, Andrew Hsiao, Leyla Mei, Rebekah Kebede, Elizabeth Mendez Berry, Deepa Fernandes . . . and the many more within the Philippines, unnamed, who continue to document and witness the unfinished revolution.

To Dr. Florentino Hornedo for pioneering Ivatan scholarship with purpose and grace. He sat and listened to our elders when few others did and spent decades bringing insight to their stories. Without his work, much more of our history would have vanished. And because of his work, many of us learned to regard our culture with love, respect and appreciation.

To the editorial and design team at Ateneo University Press for their guidance and patience during the process. And to the ADMU press reader for important feedback during revisions.

To my parents, Victor and Cynthia, for their unconditional love and belief.

To Corazon and Diom for their enthusiasm and support. And to Xochi, *milagra pequeña*, for being such a beautiful reflection of them all and so much more.

To my *kadyan* of Savidug, Chavayan, Sinakan, Vasay and throughout Batanes. A special *dyus mamahes* for your resilience, for keeping our Ivatan traditions strong, and for always finding the reasons to laugh & to sing. *Arava u ryes a abu su vinedi.*

And, finally, to Mitzi, *por todo lo que eres . . . palagi, siempre, as pirmi.*